P9-CKK-443

Bent Object
of My Affection

The Twists and Turns of Love

Terry Border

Running Press
PHILADELPHIA · LONDON

© 2011 by Terry Border
Published by Running Press,
A Member of the Perseus Books Group

All rights reserved under the Pan-American and International Copyright Conventions
Printed in China

This book may not be reproduced in whole or in part, in any form or by any means,
electronic or mechanical, including photocopying, recording, or by any information
storage and retrieval system now known or hereafter invented, without written
permission from the publisher.

Books published by Running Press are available at special discounts for bulk
purchases in the United States by corporations, institutions, and other organizations.
For more information, please contact the Special Markets Department at the
Perseus Books Group, 2300 Chestnut Street, Suite 200, Philadelphia, PA 19103, or call
(800) 810-4145, ext. 5000, or e-mail special.markets@perseusbooks.com.

ISBN 978-0-7624-4187-7
Library of Congress Control Number: 2011932182

E-book ISBN 978-0-7624-4366-6

9   8   7   6   5   4   3   2   1
Digit on the right indicates the number of this printing

Edited by Jennifer Leczkowski
Typography: Rockwell and Romy

Running Press Book Publishers
2300 Chestnut Street
Philadelphia, PA 19103-4371

Visit us on the web!
www.runningpress.com

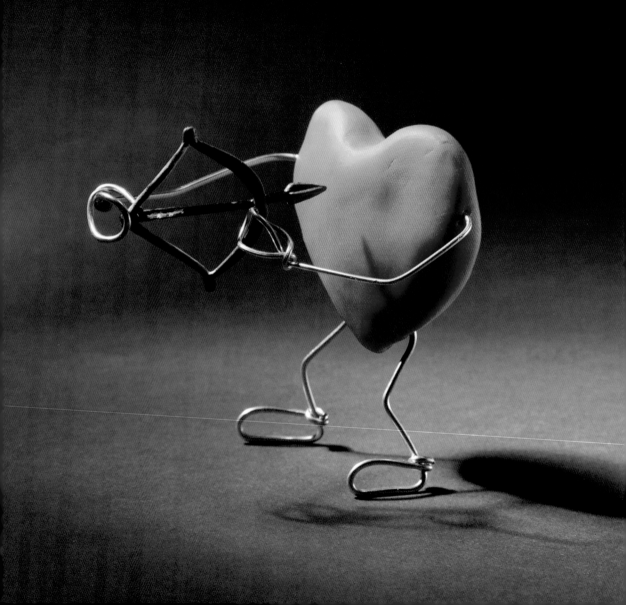

How Do I Love Thee?
Let Me Bend the Ways…

Looking for just the right words to say to that special someone, but find yourself in a pickle? Candy conversation hearts not quite capturing the mood? This collection of often sweet, sometimes twisted, but always amusing Bent Objects images is sure to express just how you feel. In a world where falling leaves can hold on to one another and spools of thread tie the knot, and where candles can light each other's fire and bananas peel it all off, *Bent Object of My Affection* shows that, like love, the ordinary can be extraordinary.

We make a perfect pair.

Straight from the Garden of Eden

I'll help
you fly and
be here
if you fall.

An Eggsellent
friendship

You let me soar, but keep me grounded.

And Then I Was the Kite and You Were the String

Together we make something bigger.

The Missing Piece

I can't help this attraction.

Magnetic Personality

You're the perfect way to start each morning.

Coffee Lovers

Olive you so much I feel tipsy.

Care for a Drink?

I love your
curves,
I love your
lumps.

Don't Go Changing

I remember the
moment
I first saw you.

Didn't We Meet in a
Pasta Life?

I'll hold on,
no matter what.

falling

I think
this could
develop
into
something.

Film Strip

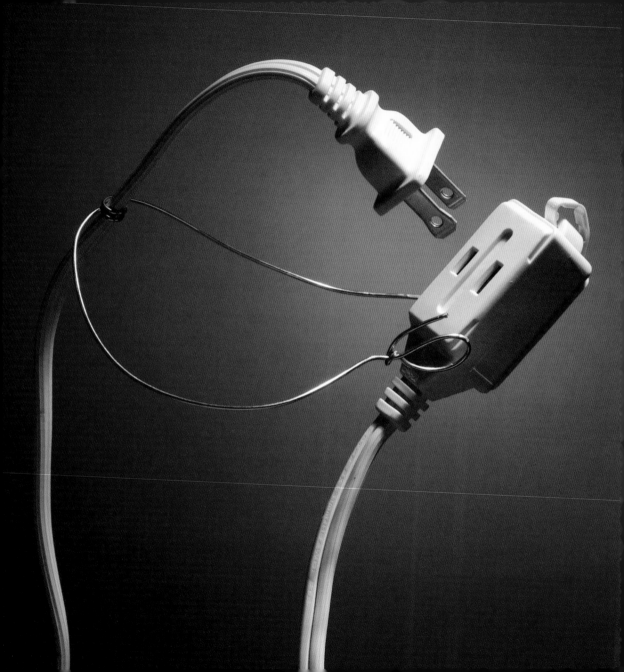

I get a charge
out of you.

Love Connection

You're irresistible.

The Cost of Being
Loved So Much

Yes, it *is* a roll of quarters in my pocket, *and* I'm glad to see you.

Is That . . ?

I love you berry much.

Honeymoon Sweet

Love me hard, we'll clean up later.

Love Is Messy

Gimme some of that sweet stuff, baby!

Pour It On

I was lucky to find you.

Shell Game

I've got
the cure for
what
ails you.

Dr. feelgood

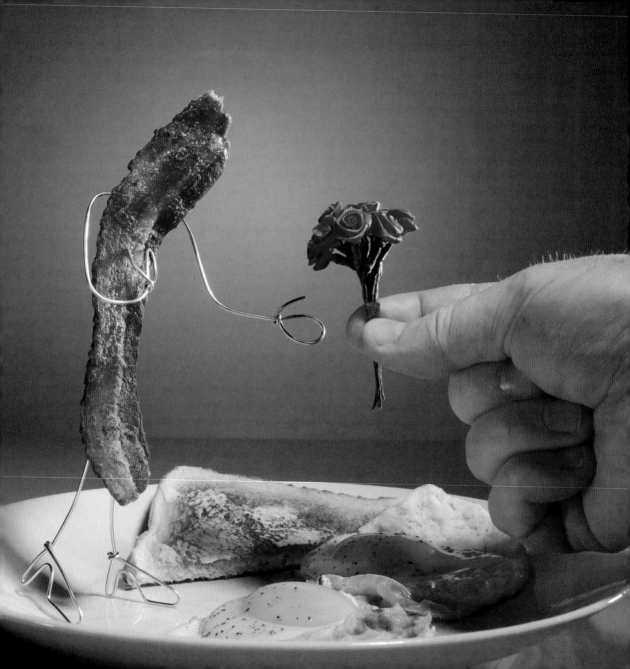

If loving you is wrong, I don't want to be right.

Unhealthy Relationship

Love is sticky.

french Kissing

You make everything a wonderland.

In the Winter We Can
Build a Doughman

Let's build our relationship.

Making Love

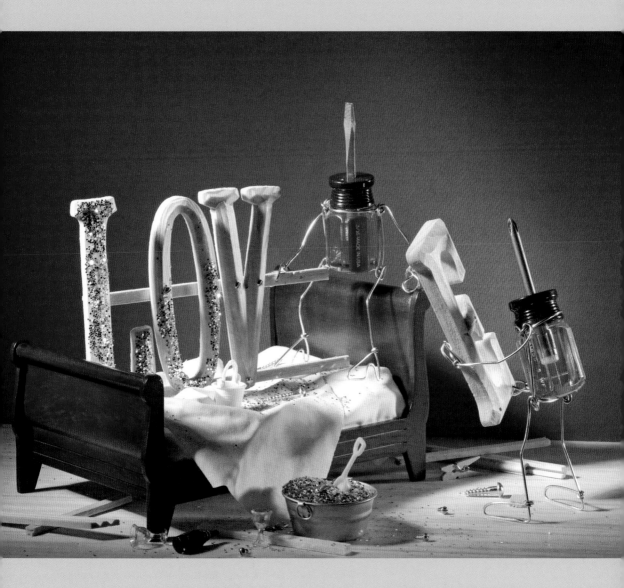

I love seeing
you nekkid.

Taking It Off

Plant one on me!

L.A. Woman

I only have dies for you.

King Leer

I love how
our lives
have
intertwined.

Tying the Knot

You're the key
to my
happiness.

Looking for the Right fit

You set me aflame.

Light My Fire

U is the object of my affection.

Be my love bird.

Sam and Ella

Wanna score?

Fiddling Around

You're the wind beneath my wings, and the breeze beneath my skirt.

Marilyn Meringue

You're the
hottest
thing I've ever
seen.

Mr. Pickle and His
Spicy Girlfriend

I want to spend every minute with you.

Quality Time

I'll keep hoping.

The Eternal Question

I love when we roll in the hay.

Butter, Anyone?

Run away with me.

The Dish and the Spoon

I've lost my
head over you.

Salome

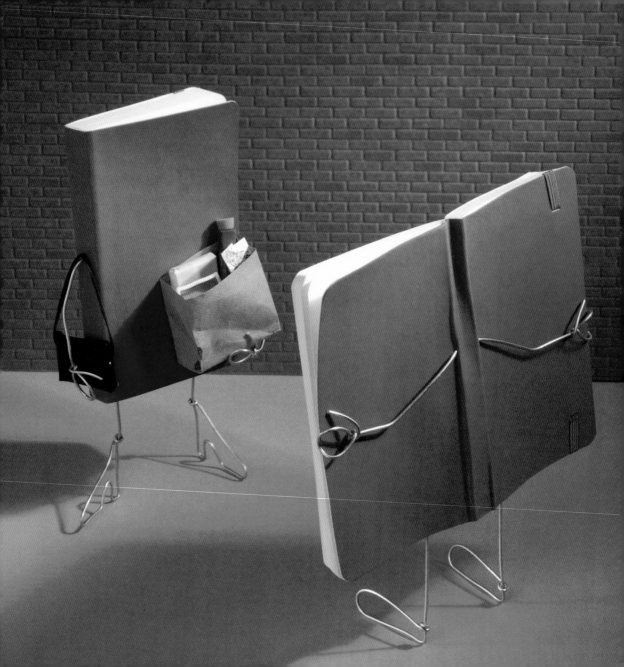

With you,
I'm an
open book.

He Always fell Open to
the Naughty Part

I love your appeal.

Undercover

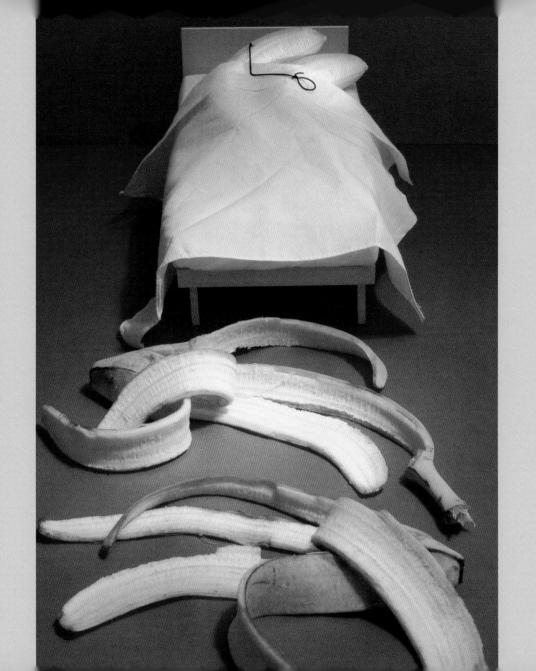

You're my comfort food.

Souper Hero

We fit so well together.

I Like It When We Spoon

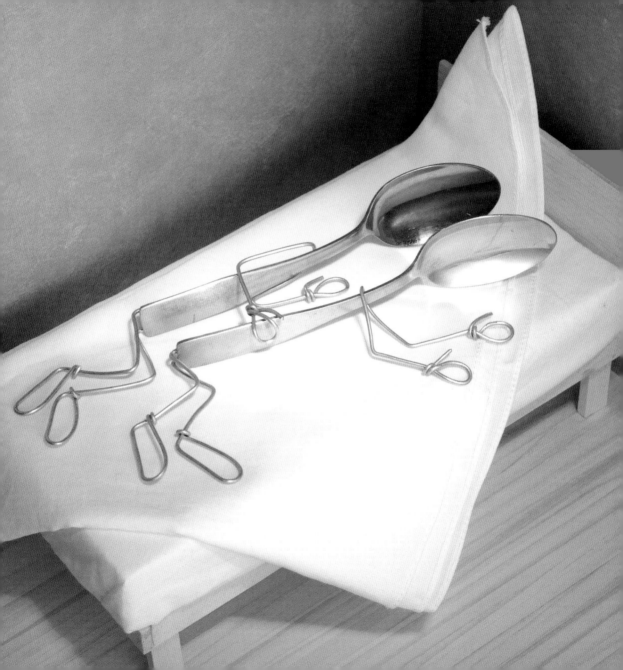

You have me licked!

Stuck On You

I love you
when you're
strong.

Studmuffin

You are the spice of my life.

Dinner Companions

You make my world go round.

Love Is free

Let's grow old together.

Shrunken and Wrinkled

You're my cherry on top.

I Scream, You Scream

I'll love you
in sickness and
in health.

Corny Moment

Don't pull the plug on me.

'Til Death Do Us Part

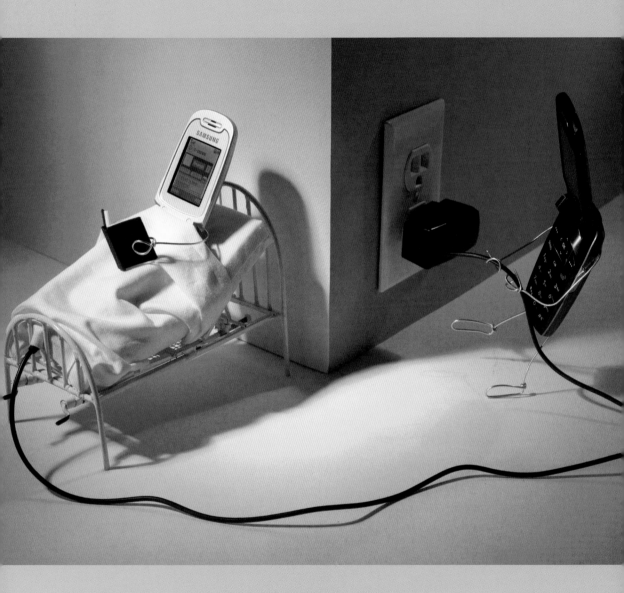

Be my Valentine.

My favorite Sweetie

I hope you're not out of my league.

Just an Ordinary Guy

It's not a party
without you.

Taking a Dip

I'd never get over you.

Misfortune Cookie

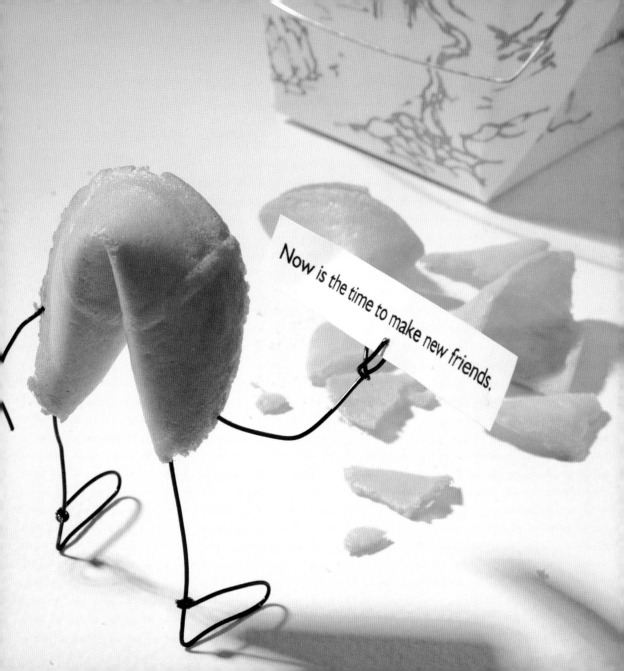

We make beautiful music.

Beans, Beans,
the Magical fruit. . .

No one else measures up.

Impressed?

I'm next in line to fall for you.

We Need a Hero

I'll love you
when
you're weak.

Yesterday's flowers

Time moves s-l-o-w-l-y when we're apart.

Without You

To Us!

A Toast